2026

THE

SHEPHERD'S ROD

BONNIE JONES

2026 The Shepherd's Rod
Copyright © 2025 Bonnie Jones

ALL RIGHTS RESERVED. This book contains material protected under International and Federal Copyright Laws and Treaties. Any unauthorized reprint or use of this material is prohibited. No part of this book may be reproduced or transmitted in any form or by any means, electronic or mechanical, including photocopying, recording, or by any information storage and retrieval system without express written permission from the author/publisher. Unless otherwise identified, Scripture quotations are taken from the New King James Version. Copyright © 1982 by Thomas Nelson, Inc. Used by permission. All rights reserved.

ISBN: 978-1-968426-21-7

CONTENTS

Introduction iii

CHAPTER ONE
OPEN DOORS OF EXPECTATION 1

CHAPTER TWO
PROPHETIC DECREES 17

CHAPTER THREE
GREATEST HARVEST OF SOULS 26

CHAPTER FOUR
WILL YOU WEAR THE GRAVE CLOTH? 37

CHAPTER FIVE
THE MARTYR'S ROBE 45

Summary 55

INTRODUCTION

The 2026 Shepherd's Rod is different from the ones I've written in previous years. This time, I felt the Lord leading me to keep it conversational; relaying His message to me and oftentimes my answers or questions back to Him. It's rather unique! Sometimes I'm in a quandary and must seek Him for greater revelation regarding the subject matter. Yet I love how He intertwines scriptural truths with mysteries untold.

> *It is the glory of God to conceal a thing, but the glory of kings is to search out a thing. (Proverbs 25:2)*

There has been a progression of doors opening over the past few years. 2024 was the "Door of Opportunity" for the bride to enter. Depending on the choice she made would determine the amount of victory she received; 30, 60 or 100-fold. Then 2025 was the "Door of Advantage" which took the body to a new level of trusting God to know what is best for them. It would set the stage for the "Door of Expectation" to open in 2026. With the opening of this door, they could expect results to happen for what they believed for.

> *Therefore, I say to you, whatever things you ask when you pray, believe that you receive them, and you will have them. (Mark 11:24)*

For those who are willing to believe for the miraculous, they will receive 100-fold. Sixty-fold goes to those who come near. But only 30-fold goes to those who lag behind; however, their faith has opportunity to grow when they believe. (Mark 5:36)

2026 is the year of prophetic decree coming to fruition. The Angel Union working with the angels that gather (Matthew 13:41) has begun to reap a great harvest in America. Jimmy Swaggart's fishing net was released following his departure to heaven July 1st. This time, there will be no snags or snares, and it will reap a great harvest of souls.

> *The Son of Man will send out His angels, and they will gather out of His kingdom all things that offend, and those who practice lawlessness. ((Matthew 13:41)*

The Lord showed me two different mantles available to the body of Christ if they are willing to pay the price. First was the grave cloth. And the question the Lord asked is, "Are you willing to wear the shame of the graves cloth?" The second is the martyr's robe. What does it mean to wear the martyr's robe? Are you willing to lay down your life for what you believe for the cross of Jesus Christ and His suffering. Both mantles will cost you everything, and not many are willing to pay the price. It's a sobering question that I believe the Father is asking all of His children.

2026 will be a year of great impact as the seeds of revival have been sown, and now the reapers go into the harvest field, laboring with angels to bring in the largest catch of souls the earth has ever seen. I pray this will be the year of great blessing, power and glory as the "Doors of Opportunity, Advantage and Expectation" have been made available for every believer to enter in Christ Jesus. Amen.

CHAPTER ONE

OPEN DOOR OF EXPECTATION

Confident Expectation

Below is a conversation I had with the Lord as He began teaching me about the "Door of Expectation" that is opening to the body of Christ. In the previous two years, He's given me a "door" that would open and the challenges that came with it. However, He also granted us the wisdom to overcome each challenge.

I want to begin this chapter with the new information regarding the "Door of Expectation," although I believe it's vital that we go back and look at the other two doors. The "Door of Opportunity" opened in 2024 and the "Door of Advantage" in 2025. I feel it's good to revisit each door to gain a greater understanding to several questions. Did we close the doors we needed to? Did we enter illegally? Did we enter with trust and a confident expectation? Let's begin with this year's revelation, and then I will add excerpts from 2024 and 2025.

Door of Expectation

The "Door of Expectation" is opening wide! Do you believe this asks God? *Yes, Lord I do. What are you saying to the body of Christ?*

It's time to not only believe for the extraordinary, it's time to expect results. The door of opportunity has been open yet few have walked through. Why? They didn't believe they could. Some came near yet only a few received. Their faith needs to be exercised today. Now for those who are willing to believe for the miraculous they are going to receive 100-fold. Sixty-fold goes to those who come near while only thirty-fold to those who lag behind. **Their faith has opportunity to grow when they believe.**

> *As soon as Jesus heard the word that was spoken, He said to the ruler of the synagogue, "Do not be afraid; only believe." (Mark 5:36)*

The mind has over ruled the spirit of man so long, it dominates his thinking and as he thinks so he does. Now I'm opening this door wide and you are going to step through with wild imagination and expectation. **What you say will be – if you only believe. Believe in Me not man and not self.**

Believe that you already have the desire I've place in your heart and receive it. Amen.

Moses believed and he received the Ten Commandments. He believed he could see Me face to face and he believed he could lead Israel out of bondage. He believed I AM could deliver them. In his own ability he could not, but when he believed in the One who could, he did.

Now I say to you today, look no further for your answers, you already have them. The world of evangelism will open wide by faith in the One who delivers. And words of faith will ignite a fire with the sword of power. Now go and open doors of expectation for others as you deliver this message of hope. In Jesus name. Amen.

Year of Open Doors of Opportunity
Excerpt from 2024 Shepherd's Rod

2024 is the Year of Open Doors of Opportunity! This is an invitation to enter through three open doors in the Book of Revelation. On the Day of Atonement, the Lord asked me, "Who is willing and who is ready to step through these doors? Are you? Do you love the Lord with all your heart and serve His Kingdom? Have you placed yourself upon the mercy seat for others, not yourself?" These are the questions the Lord asked me, and I answered each one. Yet I asked Him to tell me because only He knows the true intent of my heart. And I believe He is asking His Bride these questions today and each one must answer for oneself. This invitation is not only an opportunity to dine with Him, but to boldly enter the throne room of heaven where mysteries are revealed.

The Lord said, "You are going to see many challenges in the coming year but each one carries a greater reward of value as you conquer each one. Know this, the challenge is the enemy's way of trying to prevent you from succeeding in Me. However, you are already equipped with success and must walk past each roadblock and barrier he sets before you. They are not mountains; no, they are mole hills. They are only mountains if you lose perspective of the success you already are in Me. Conquer each one with love and confidence and continue walking." Amen.

I always appreciate when the Lord gives me a head's up especially when He forewarns me of the enemy's plan. Sometimes it's vague and other times it's detailed, but I know the enemy's objective is to derail what God has planned for good. I realize there will be challenges but we have already been equipped with every good thing we need to succeed in Him. If God is for me who can be against me? (Romans 8:31) I've been given all kingdom authority and walk in its power and might. (Matthew 28:18-20) I am the head and not the tail, (Deuteronomy 28:13) and no weapon formed against me shall prosper, (Isaiah 54:17) for greater is He who is in me than he who is in this world. (1 John 4:4) The devil is a defeated foe and he knows it. We cannot take a back seat to him; we must advance forward in power and might!

The Lord said, "Doors of opportunity are opening for His bride to enter through. She's being given choices to make and depending on the choice she makes will determines the amount of victory she receives - thirty, sixty or a hundredfold. You see not everyone who enters through the door shall receive a hundredfold. The victory comes according to obedience and inheritance."

First, they must hear God's voice and obey, then they can enter through the door of opportunity. There are many doors, and one leads to another. Some people will think this is it. Some will stop and set up camp, but then stop listening. Yet the wise ones indulge in blessings where they camp but continue to listen and obey. They will then have opportunity to move on through the next door and so on.

There are also times we receive thirtyfold blessings and at other times sixty or a hundredfold. I believe that all born again Christians live in the blessings of God. We are the seed of Abraham the father of faith and therefore entitled to receive spiritual blessings. Many of them are tied to the land we possess. No matter where our physical location is we remain blessed. However, being in the right location increases our ability to receive more abundantly. We may receive thirtyfold in one location yet in another a hundredfold where it seems like the blessings are chasing us down. If we relocate and become complacent, by our own hand we limit our blessing and therefore only receive thirtyfold. That's why it's important we continue to hear and obey and not let our guard down. We must be willing to leave Haran for Beersheba.

God is not short in blessing His children. However, they are short in hearing and shorter yet in obeying. Some become complacent and comfy in their camp. Many have followed man's voice and it caused them to be in the wrong place for seasons in their life. But God is speaking loud and clear to those who have an ear to hear. Let there be no mistake, He's uprooting many and bringing them into the land of plenty. Some have been in dry and arid places, but that's about to change. And what was dry for one will be an oasis for another.

Open Doors in Revelation

The last open door in Scripture is Revelations 4:1, it's the one at the beginning of this chapter. Bob Jones always said that the Book of Revelation is a love letter to His Bride. Although the next two open doors were written to the Churches of Philadelphia and Laodicea, I believe they represent the refining process the remnant goes through to receive an invitation to the "open door" of Revelation 4:1.

> *Philadelphia - These things says He who is holy, He who is true, "He who has the key of David, He who opens and no one shuts, and shuts and no one opens." "I know your works. See, I have set before you an open door, and no one can shut it; for you have a little strength, have kept My word, and have not denied My name. (Revelation 3:7-8)*

To the remnant of Philadelphia, He who is holy and true, holds the "Key of David" (Isaiah 22:22) and Christ alone has authority to open this door. He alone prevents anyone else from closing it. There are three conditions in Revelation 3:9 that qualify them. First, they have little strength which means they live by faith. James 2:24 says that a man is justified by works, and not by faith only. Yet the remnant's faith works through love. (Galatians 5:6) Second, they have kept His Word; therefore, they did not compromise the Gospel. And third, they have not denied His name, His name is Love. (1John 4:8) Therefore, Love holds the "Key of David" to unlock this door so the faithful remnant who abides in Love (John 15:20) may proceed.

Laodicea - As many as I love, I rebuke and chasten. Therefore, be zealous and repent. Behold, I stand at the door and knock. If anyone hears My voice and opens the door, I will come in to him and dine with him, and he with Me. To him who overcomes I will grant to sit with Me on My throne, as I also overcame and sat down with My Father on His throne. (Revelation 3:19-21)

Only Christ could open the first door, and it was the remnant's faith working through Love that put them in position to gain more access. However, the Laodicean remnant contains overcomers because they overcome the lukewarm spirit. When He chastised them for their lukewarm Christianity, they quickly repented. Now they're granted permission to open the door because the Lord is standing on the other side and knocking. But the key is this, they must be attentive to hear His voice and open it. And because they did, they're invited to come in and dine with Him and granted permission to sit down with Papa on His throne.

Throne Room of Heaven

After these things I looked, and behold, a door standing open in heaven. And the first voice which I heard was like a trumpet speaking with me, saying, "Come up here, and I will show you things which must take place after this." (Revelation 4:1)

Jesus opened the door to the faithful remnant. It was their faith working through Love that gave them access. After the Laodicean remnant repented and overcame their lukewarmness He knocked on their door with a dinner invitation in His hand. There's a progression taking place here. Because of the remnant's faith that works through Love, Jesus opens the door of opportunity. And it is here that a greater level of faith is required. After the Lord's rebuke the remnant must do a thorough self-examination. He said, "You are neither cold nor hot. But because you are lukewarm, I will vomit you out of My mouth. Because you say, 'I am rich, have become wealthy, and have need of nothing' and do not know that you are wretched, miserable, poor, blind, and naked." (Revelation 3:15-17) But He said, "I know your works!" Their works by faith got them thus far but there's a lot of baggage attached. Because He loves them, He corrects them. He said, "As many as I love, I rebuke and chasten. Therefore, be zealous and repent." (Revelation 3:19) Their love for Him caused them to repent quickly which qualified them for entrance to this door.

This is the bride's invitation to enter the throne room of heaven. The door is standing open and there is no need to knock. There is nothing to prevent the remnant from entering through this door. This is where the Bride of Christ rests in Holy Spirit and receives pertinent revelation. Here is where wisdom and understanding reside and spiritual knowledge is imparted. Mysteries of Scripture are understood and released to the remnant's spirit. The throne room is open and available for the remnant who has an ear to hear what the Spirit is saying to the churches of Revelation. And all who enter shall join the angels who worship day and night saying, "Holy, holy, holy, Lord God Almighty, Who was and is and is to come!" (Revelation 4:8b)

Door of Advantage Will Open
Excerpts from 2025 Shepherd's Rod

Therefore, your gates shall be open continually; They shall not be shut day or night. Isaiah 60:11a)

This year the "Door of Advantage" will open, (1 Cor. 16:9) and ones must enter through with expectation, My expectation. They cannot flippantly enter. They enter by trusting Me, that I know what's best, what's true and what's significant for their life. Trust is moving on a whole new level in this season. They must learn to trust Me not their own thoughts and feelings and not trusting friends or the internet. They must trust Almighty God who created them.

> *Trust in the Lord with all your heart and lean not on your own understanding; in all your ways acknowledge Him, And He shall direct your paths. (Proverbs 3:5-6)*

We must respond to the effect of the door that opens to our advantage. Last year the "Door of Opportunity" opened which created a set of circumstances making it possible for us to do something. The Lord was setting the stage for this year's "Door of Advantage" to open. For this advantage is now favorable to help us succeed in what He has called us to do. In 1 Corinthians 16:9, Paul says that a great door for effective work has opened to him, yet there are many who opposed him and his work. This signifies that while Paul is experiencing a significant opportunity to spread the Gospel, he also faced considerable opposition. It was to Paul's advantage to take the opportunity to remain faithful to the cross and face the challenges. We must realize the bigger the door, the more resistance we might encounter.

> *For a great and effective door has opened to me, and there are many adversaries. (1 Cor. 16:9)*

Last year we had choices to make as we entered through the "Doors of Opportunity." Depending on the choice we made it would determine the amount of victory we received - thirty, sixty or a hundredfold. The victory was determined according to our obedience and inheritance. This year the Lord said, "When My beloved enters the "Door of Advantage," old things will pass away and they shall see My light shine upon their future. It's a door of advantage but if they don't enter by trust in Me, it will be to their disadvantage, and they will return empty handed." I believe this offer remains available as the bride is maturing in her calling and her level of obedience.

Looking Back

Perhaps we should look back to 2024 and the doors of opportunity we entered. To walk through a door of opportunity, we had to be willing to close the one behind us. What did that look like? It would be different for each one of us. What was God requiring of you to give up, lay down or surrender to Him? For some it could have been financial, perhaps to begin tithing to the local church. For others it could have been a geographical move, leaving the familiar behind. While others had to lay down addictions such as alcohol, drugs or cigarettes. Some had to give up pornography, unhealthy relationships, or foul language. Perhaps laying down food addictions, binge-watching TV, video games or surfing the net. Many had to let go of a lost loved one and turn them over to God trusting Him with their life. Some had to close the door to a bad marriage or abusive relationship.

Some had to sacrifice a job promotion to care for an elderly parent. The list could go on and on. Many doors that the body of Christ chose to close were extremely painful and costly. There's a wide variety of things God has dealt with in the body of Christ. As each one gave it up, laid it down or surrendered it to Christ, they did so because their love for Him is far greater than the vice that held them captive and prevented them from moving onward and upward in Him. It was like carrying around a ball and chain with each step they took. The Lord wanted His bride free from all hindrances and not to carry any baggage through the door of opportunity. He wants His bride free of the junk she's been dabbling with so she can receive fresh oil in this next season. He wants her to be holy as He is holy.

> *But as the One Who called you is holy, you yourselves also be holy in all your conduct and manner of living. For it is written, you shall be holy, for I am holy. (1 Peter 1:15-16)*

It was our decision to give it up, lay it down or surrender it to Him. It was our decision to close that negative offensive door. And once we repented with a sincere heart, and closed it behind us, the Lord opened our "door of opportunity." Some repented quickly, laying down their agenda while others took a while. The sooner we laid it down and walked through the door of opportunity the sooner we begin to reap our harvest of thirty, sixty or a hundredfold. Now in this season we have the advantage to become successful in what God called us to. Some of us died a painful death going through the door of opportunity. It's not always pleasant to give up something you enjoyed for a long time. But once you did, it's behind you and now it's to your advantage to keep our eyes on the cross while walking in His holiness and truth. For the Lord has called us to be like Him. He has called us to be set apart from the world because He's called us into a holy consecration. In Leviticus 20:7 He tells the children of Israel, "Consecrate yourselves therefore and be holy; for I am the Lord your God. There was a cleansing that needed to take place among them.

In the same way today, we are to be separated from the world by the blood of Jesus, because we are citizens of the Kingdom of God and He's called us into His holiness. Leviticus 20:26 says, "And you shall be holy to Me; for I the Lord am holy, and have separated you from the peoples, that you should be Mine. He's called us to holiness in Him; daily consecrating ourselves to His purpose through His gift of salvation on the cross.

> *For God has not called us to impurity but to consecration [to dedicate ourselves to the most thorough purity]. (1 Thessalonians 4:7)*

Understanding the Door of Expectation

What are God's personal promises to you? What have you been patiently waiting for? What are you willing to believe for? All your promises in Him are yes and amen. (2 Corinthians 1:20) Are you willing to believe for the extraordinary? Or are you like the disciples that Christ rebuked for their little faith? (Matthew 8:26) Are you willing to step out of the boat? Are you willing to have radical faith and trust God completely? Can you believe and not doubt? Are you ready for the greater works to manifest in your life? (John 14:12)

> *For this reason, I am telling you, whatever you ask for in prayer, believe (trust and be confident) that it is granted to you, and you will [get it]. (Mark 11:24AMPC)*

The term "Expecting" describes a woman who is pregnant and anticipating the birth of her child. I believe the body of Christ has been long anticipating the birthing of her child of promise. They've had a confident expectation for many years and now the seed of Abraham, the father of our faith is about to burst forth in a new dimension.

In these past seasons our faith has been stretched and strengthened. We had to learn to walk by faith, and not by sight. We had to learn to trust the Lord with all our heart, and not lean on our own understanding. We had to trust the Lord for every measure of hope. And now it's time to believe and receive, with great expectation, the hope of glory. It's time to believe for the extraordinary to be ordinary and keep our eyes on Christ. It's time to reach into the eternal hope of glory. We must look beyond the natural realm and step over the threshold through the door of expectation.

I believe that where the body has lacked confidence in the past now the door of expectation will open, and you will step through it. And once you do, you will have a greater level of belief in the promises of yes and amen.

I believe the bride has moved beyond the "door of opportunity", through the "door of advantage" and now stepping over the threshold of the "door of expectation". Get ready for your extraordinary journey to begin. Get ready to go beyond the limits of your imagination.

Confident Expectation

We do not boast therefore, beyond our proper limit, over other men's labors, but we have the hope and confident expectation that as your faith continues to grow, our field among you may be greatly enlarged, still within the limits of our commission. (2 Corinthians 10:15 AMPC)

CHAPTER TWO

PROPHETIC DECREES

Angel Union

Although I won't go into all the details now regarding my move to Indiana, I want to unfold a story that not only revealed a clue as to where I would relocate, it also gave me understanding that this "new thing" God is doing is much greater than I anticipated. And I get to be a part of it.

On May 21, 2025, I was at my son's house in Pennsylvania to celebrate my daughter's surprise birthday party. Afterwards I spent the night and would return home to South Carolina the following day. Just after midnight I had a prophetic dream with Bob Jones. In the dream Bob was seated in the front passenger seat of a white van while I was standing outside next to his window. With a stern voice he said, "Take me to Union County." Immediately I walked around to the driver side to get in and drive him; however, he was now seated in the driver seat with both hands firmly on the steering wheel. He was looking straight ahead very intently. I asked him two times to scoot over so I could get in. Each time he never flinched nor did he answer. He kept his hands firm on the steering wheel and stared straight ahead. He did not budge. I realized he represented either Jesus, or Holy Spirit, who is driving this vehicle, and I was only going along for the ride. I needed to get into the passenger seat and let Him do the driving. And we must remember this, Holy Spirit MUST be the one directing our path. We MUST allow Him to lead us while we simply obey and therefore just go along for the ride.

When I arrived back home the next day, I began researching Union County in America. To my surprise, there are 17 states with a Union County. I wondered which state He was indicating to me. Thinking perhaps He was relocating me to "Union County" in one of the 17 states. About a week later, while having lunch with a friend, I remembered Bob stating that the angel over America's name is Union. I realized what God is doing in America is far greater than I anticipated.

In the wee hours of the morning on June 7, the Lord began speaking to me regarding the Angel Union. What I've listed below are the decrees I made following the Lord's direction. I feel each decree is vital to what is taking place in the United States currently. And not only now but in the days to come. Since it involves 17 states, 17 is a number of God's divine order. I believe the Lord has strategically placed true believers in the resurrected Christ in positions of authority throughout America. They are ones who will not compromise the cross of Jesus Christ. And this is far greater than I can imagine. However. my desire is to follow Him and complete my part of what He's called me to do. I believe each member of the army He's called together for this purpose will walk in truth, honor, love and integrity. And they will never compromise but march forward in the power and authority of the Lord.

June 7, 2025

This was a busy night. I had gone to the bathroom and went back to bed and began to pray. Praying for the president and current situations in America. Then I felt the presence of the Lord and begin hearing, praying and writing. Here's what followed.

3:25 AM
Let the Angel Union over America cast his fishing net from North to South and East to West and let him drape it from border to border.

Let the harvest of America's souls begin. Let not one soul be lost to the Kingdom of darkness. Amen.

Let the Angel Union bring with him the winnowing fork and winnow the wheat and chaff.

> *His winnowing fan is in His hand, and He will thoroughly clean out His threshing*

> *floor, and gather His wheat into the barn; but He will burn up the chaff with unquenchable fire." (Matthew 3:12)*

Let Union be once again united in America from sea to shining sea.

Lord, let every harvester arise this day and take their position. Put angels around each one to guide, guard and protect them and their families until each soul You've assigned them is brought into the Kingdom of light.

Lord, let the Kingdom of darkness suffer loss as the Kingdom of light invades it.

> *But you, brethren, are not in darkness, so that this Day should overtake you as a thief. You are all sons of light and sons of the day. We are not of the night nor of darkness. (1 Thessalonians 5:4-5)*

Let there be sorrow and gnashing of teeth as the Kingdom of darkness's gates are closed and draped with blood-stained memories of past victories.

> *The Son of Man will send out His angels, and they will gather out of His kingdom all things that offend, and those who practice lawlessness, and will cast them into the furnace of fire. There will be*

> *wailing and gnashing of teeth. Then the righteous will shine forth as the sun in the kingdom of their Father. He who has ears to hear, let him hear! (Matthew 13:41-43)*

Lord, let the Angel Union bring holiness back into this nation.

> *But as He who called you is holy, you also be holy in all your conduct, because it is written, "Be holy, for I am holy," (1 Peter 1:15-16) and (Leviticus 19:2)*

Let honor and solidarity be established in this nation as unity among the brethren is reinstated.

> *Behold, how good and how pleasant it is for brethren to dwell together in unity! (Psalm 133:1)*

Let love for one another and honor be the driving force in this great movement of Union's authority.

> *And you shall love the LORD your God with all your heart, with all your soul, with all your mind, and with all your strength. This is the first commandment. And the second, like it, is this: You shall love your neighbor as yourself. There is no other commandment greater than these. (Mark 12:30-31)*

Let angel Union not rest until America is reaped and delivered from darkness. In Jesus name I ask according to Thy will oh Lord. Amen and Amen.

Lord, let the Angels Promise and Hope and Peace and Harmony work with Angel Union to complete the reaping of America. Lord, let America's borders be closed to strangers and let the evil intruders return to their own countries. In Jesus name. Amen. 3:39 AM

Note: I put down my pen and turned off the lamp on the night stand, but only momentarily as the Lord began speaking again.

3:54 AM
Lord, let the olive branch return to America.

In the Bible, an olive branch symbolizes peace, reconciliation, and new beginnings. It's most famously associated with Noah's Ark, where a dove returned with an olive leaf after the flood, signifying the end of judgment and the promise of a renewed world. The olive tree itself is also a symbol of prosperity, fertility, and divine blessing.

Let America be saved. Let her people rejoice in Thy holy name.

Let the angels stand guard and not retreat until the trumpet sounds!

Let freedom ring on every shore.

Let all the nations rejoice.

Let Egypt leave, and Israel arise.

I believe the Lord is speaking here of Egypt representing the systems of this world and Israel is the spiritual system. And His children being aligned with God and His kingdom of Light. The Kingdom of Light must arise and blot out, diminish and dismantle the kingdom of darkness.

Let freedom ring forth. Amen.

Note: There was silence for a moment, then He continued.

There's a cooing of the dove taking place in America this day.

As in the days of Noah, the dove represents renewal, purity and Holy Spirit.

> *The flowers appear on the earth; The time of singing has come, And the voice of the turtledove is heard in our land. (SOS 2:12)*

She is bringing home the lost ones,

The soul of unrest is now abounding.

The dry bones are rattling and coming forth,
Breath is being revived in the soul of man's desire.

Let the dry bones arise with the blood of the Lamb,
And their nostrils be filled with holiness. Amen.

Let there be light from above to fill every bone with power,
And illuminate the soul's darkness.

Let the marrow of these bones breathe God's breath and live!
Bone of His bone and flesh of His flesh forever and ever. Amen.

> *So, I prophesied as I was commanded; and as I prophesied, there was a noise, and suddenly a rattling; and the bones came together, bone to bone. Indeed, as I looked the sinews and the flesh came upon them, and the skin covered them over; but there was no breath in them.*
>
> *Also, He said to me, "Prophesy to the breath, prophesy, son of man, and say to the breath, 'Thus says the Lord GOD: "Come from the four winds, O breath, and breathe on these slain, that they may live." So, I prophesied as He*

*commanded me, and breath came into them,
and they lived, and stood upon their feet, an
exceedingly great army. (Ezekiel 37:7-10)*

Note: Once again, I placed my pen on the nightstand, but only for a second as He continued speaking.

4:00 AM
Let this decree go forth this day from here throughout eternity.

Let Your word be established, Lord God, and let Your freedom be. Amen and Amen.

> *So shall My word be that goes forth from
> My mouth; It shall not return to Me void,
> but it shall accomplish what I please, and it
> shall prosper in the thing for which I sent
> it. (Isaiah 55:11)*

For where the Spirit of the Lord is there is liberty.

> *Now the Lord is the Spirit; and where the
> Spirit of the Lord is, there is liberty.
> (2 Corinthians 3:17)*

Let your freedom and justice be established in America this day. Amen and Amen.

Righteousness and justice are the foundation of Your throne. (Psalm 89:14)

Stand fast therefore in the liberty by which Christ has made us free, and do not be entangled again with a yoke of bondage. (Galatians 5:1)

Understanding the Decrees

I believe each of these prophetic decrees are significant in their own right. Each one stands alone, yet they dovetail with the others. This is a culmination of time and seasons, and the angel over America "Union" has been given permission, power and authority to reap the long-awaited harvest of America.

If you are born again into Christ, you have a significant role to play in this harvest. Every word you speak has power and might, it can be used for good or for evil. (Proverbs 18:21) That's why it's vital that we bring our mind into agreement with Christ, (Romans 12:2) and bridle our tongue. (James 1:26) Therefore only releasing what God gives us to speak.

> *Death and life are in the power of the tongue, and those who love it will eat its fruit. (Proverbs 18:21)*

We are not AI generated; we are children of the great I AM. We carry His DNA and walk in Kingdom power and authority. It is in this time that we must co-labor with the angels that gather in Matthew 13:41-42.

> *The Son of Man will send out His angels, and they will gather out of His kingdom all things that offend, and those who practice lawlessness, and will cast them into the furnace of fire. There will be wailing and gnashing of teeth. (Matthew 13:41-42)*

It is time we arise and shine, and let the glory of God shine through us (Isaiah 60:1-2) to distinguish the brilliance of His glorious light in this dark world. Let Holy Spirit be the driving force, and you go along for this ride into the harvest field where your name is written. Let us join our faith with Christ and reap the harvest Christ died for. Let us bear his shame as we walk victorious in His name. Amen.

CHAPTER THREE

GREATEST HARVEST OF SOULS

All Things MUST Come Into Proper Alignment

Everything God does is in perfect time, season, and order. Below, I have a timeline that I believe God has ordained for the greatest harvest of souls the earth has ever known. Although I believe this great harvest began some years ago, in a small measure, I believe it will now increase and multiply, and there will be no end.

In Chapter Two I listed many prophetic decrees the Lord gave me on June 7. However, I'm listing some of them again in this chapter because I feel they are significant to the timeline of the harvest. You will see as this chapter unfolds the importance to each degree.

*Let the Angel Union over America cast his fishing net from North to South and East to West and let him drape it from border to border.

*Let the harvest of America's souls begin. Let not one soul be lost to the Kingdom of darkness. Amen.

*Let the Angel Union bring with him the winnowing fork and winnow the wheat and chaff.

*Let Union be once again united in America from sea to shining sea.

*Lord, let every harvester arise this day and take their position. Put angels around each one to guide, guard and protect them and their families until each soul You've assigned them is brought into the Kingdom of light.

*Lord, let the Angel Union bring holiness back into this nation.

*Let love for one another and honor be the driving force in this great movement of Union's authority.

*Let Angel Union not rest until America is reaped and delivered from darkness. In Jesus name I ask according to Thy will oh Lord. Amen and Amen.

Jimmy Swaggart's Fishing Net

Exactly 8 days following the prophetic decrees, on Father's Day June 15, Jimmy Swaggart suffered a cardiac arrest. Apparently, he never regained consciousness and went home to Jesus July 1st.

Many years ago, the Lord showed Bob Jones, a huge fishing net. Bob said it was the largest net he'd ever seen. The Lord asked Bob who did he believe it belonged to. Bob's response was the Apostle Paul because many believed in Christ because of Paul's gospel. But the Lord told Bob it was Jimmy Swaggart's fishing net and that he had reaped the greatest harvest of souls for the kingdom. However, Jimmy Swaggart's fishing net got snagged and lost. But the Lord promised Bob that after Jimmy Swaggart's death, it would be found once again and cast out over the sea of restless humanity.

I believe this was the seed of evangelism that was sown into the ground on July 1 with Jimmy Swaggart's departure to heaven. There have been many evangelists who have won souls for the kingdom, but with this great fishing net being cast once again, it will be the greatest reaping of lost souls the world has ever known.

Shot Heard Around the World

On September 10, there was a shot heard around the world with the assassination of Charlie Kirk. Because of his influence around the globe, the stage was set in every corner of the world for a single shot to be echoed worldwide. Within moments, Charlie Kirk became a household name. His name was on the lips of millions and prayer vigils began immediately worldwide. We lost a leader, a friend and a fellow soldier in the army of the Lord. Charlie's life was dedicated to turning America back to God, to justice and freedom and truth. He often said, "If you believe in something, you need to have the courage to fight for those ideas, not run away from them, or try and silence them."

Needless Casualty of War

Many people have commented on the assassination of Charlie Kirk - some good and some evil. Some have been mean spirited but God judges the heart of man. He did more in 31 years than most people who live a long life. God's grace was upon him to accomplish all the things he did.

I sought the Lord about this – *Why did this happen?*

The Lord spoke this to me, "Charlie Kirk's death was predestined and yes, a needless casualty of war. But you must understand, his life was complete. In his death, more will turn to Me than in his life. Sound strange?" *No, I think I understand.*

The Lord said, "People mourn heroes and rise up for justice. This is what his life was all about. My eye is upon the sparrow; nothing gets away from Me. This is not over, says God. I am the Way and the only way, and in this day, you will witness justice applied. Only a few have totally surrendered to the extent Charlie Kirk did and dedicated their entire life to Me with selfless ambition. I appointed him once to die for Me to expand My Kingdom, and he did."

Truly I tell you, unless a grain of wheat falls to the ground and dies, it remains by itself. But if it dies, it produces much fruit. (John 12:24)

There were 17,000 chapters of Turning Point USA at the time of his death. Today there are 62,000 chapters and growing daily.

My Prayer

Thank you, Lord, for this word today. Let us as a nation turn back to You with a whole heart. Let Charlie Kirk's death be a turning point for America. Let us as a nation see Your hand in this and focus on Your divine plan and purpose for America and beyond. In Jesus name. Amen.

The Lord's response, "I love America, and I allowed this to happen to sow a seed of righteousness for My namesake and reunite America on their own soil. Oh yes, many object to him, they oppose Me too. Let their hearts be hardened still as one by one they are eliminated from service and others taken home. Yes, the home they chose with their heart and confessed with their mouth. In Jesus holy name. Amen."

End-Time Harvest of Souls

2020 began the "Decade of the Mouth" and it started with the Covid pandemic. Everyone being required to wear a face mask to keep their mouth covered. The enemy was trying to keep us silent. But here we are 5 years later. The mask is something of the past and we have grace to speak what God has placed in our heart and on our tongue. The mask has been removed, no longer is our voice silenced. And there's an urgency to arise and shine (Isaiah 60:1) and allow your voice to be heard.

> *For this is he who was spoken of by the prophet Isaiah, saying: "The voice of one crying in the wilderness: 'Prepare the way of the LORD; Make His paths straight.' (Matthew 3:3)*

We are commanded as followers of Christ, to be His disciples and go into all the nations, preaching the gospel, healing the sick, raising the dead and casting out demons. (Matthew 10:8 & 28:18-19) If we are true followers of the living God, then we must not cower or compromise. We must go, and be about our Father's business.

We should be greatly honored that God has chosen

us to be alive at this time in church history. He has chosen the finest wine for the end times. As soldiers of the cross, let's seek Him daily for our living bread, and follow His divine order to reap the greatest harvest of souls. God is an equal opportunity employer. Each of His children will receive daily impartation if they are willing to receive it.

The "Door of Expectation" is open wide, who will dare to walk through it? Will you? What is God requiring of you? Dare to believe and walk into your destiny in Him. Co-labor with the living God and expect the extraordinary to be ordinary.

And He said to them, come after Me [as disciples—letting Me be your Guide], follow Me, and I will make you fishers of men! (Matthew 4:19 AMPC)

CHAPTER FOUR

WILL YOU WEAR THE GRAVE CLOTH?

Become A Victor

Another conversation the Lord had with me was understanding Jesus' grave cloths. Honest, I haven't given it much thought over the years. Seems like the resurrection story focuses on Christ rising from the grave, the surprise of the women and interaction with the angels. Little is said about the grave cloths with the exception that the face cloth (handkerchief) was separate from the body cloths. In fact, I've never heard anyone teach or preach about them. But I feel it's important to the Lord and this is one of those hidden treasures He's sharing with His bride.

> *Now the first day of the week, Mary Magdalene went to the tomb early, while it was still dark, and saw that the stone had been taken away from the tomb. Then she ran and came to Simon Peter, and to the other disciple, whom Jesus loved, and said to them, "They have taken away the Lord out of the tomb, and we do not know where they have laid Him."*

Peter therefore went out, and the other disciple, and were going to the tomb. So, they both ran together, and the other disciple outran Peter and came to the tomb first. And he, stooping down and looking in, saw the linen cloths lying there; yet he did not go in. Then Simon Peter came, following him, and went into the tomb; and he saw the linen cloths lying there, and the handkerchief that had been around His head, not lying with the linen cloths, but folded together in a place by itself. Then the other disciple, who came to the tomb first, went in also; and he saw and believed. For as yet they did not know the Scripture, that He must rise again from the dead. Then the disciples went away again to their own homes. (John 20:1-10)

New life and new stride. You will be amazed. Now go to this day and focus on Me and **become a victor of the grave cloths**.

Bonnie, do you realize the power that was in them? *No, I haven't thought about that Lord.* Well, consider this; they were on My body when I was resurrected. The power, the residue remained. What did they do with them? *I don't know Lord.*

Mary kept them, she removed them and later buried them so no one else would steal them. They remain entombed yet today. Oh yes years have decayed them into the earth but I'm going to resurrect them in the body of believers. And today I'm starting with you. **Will you wear the grave cloth asks God?** *Lord, I don't know what do you mean?* **Will you wear the shame for the body of Christ and dwell in the shame of the grave for them?** *If that is what You call me to do yes, I will.*

Wearing the shame of the grave cloth. What exactly does it mean and who wore them? Who in Scripture was persecuted more than the Apostle Paul. Five times he received 39 stripes; he was beaten with rods and stoned three times. He was shipwrecked, beaten, robbed, snake bit, left for dead and the list continues. (Read 2 Corinthians 11:22-29) But he did all this for the glory of God. He wanted nothing more than to know Christ and Him crucified. (1 Corinthians 2:1-3)

> *And I, brethren, when I came to you, did not come with excellence of speech or of wisdom declaring to you the testimony of God. For I determined not to know anything among you except Jesus Christ and Him crucified. I was with you in weakness, in fear, and in much trembling. (1 Corinthians 2:1-3)*

Remember, Galatians 2:20, Paul declared his crucifixion with Christ having become dead to sin in his body, he became one in union with Christ. However, his spirit man remained in a fleshly body and vulnerable to the sin nature. By faith in Christ, Paul trusted the Lord to guide and direct him in every area of life. It was no longer Paul's life, it was Christ' life being lived out through Paul's obedience to the cross and willingly allowing his flesh to be crucified daily.

> *I have been crucified with Christ; it is no longer I who live, but Christ lives in me; and the life which I now live in the flesh I live by faith in the Son of God, who loved me and gave Himself for me. (Galatians 2:20)*

Paul's lack of compromise of the Gospel and Christ's cross often times caused pain and suffering in his flesh. Yet he remained bold in Christ and endured the race set before him, keeping his eyes on Jesus, the author and finisher of his faith. And with joy in Christ' sufferings, not his own, despised the shame of the cross that bore the sin of all mankind.

> *Therefore we also, since we are surrounded by so great a cloud of witnesses, let us lay aside every weight, and the sin which so easily ensnares us, and let us run with endurance the race that is set before us, looking unto Jesus, the author*

and finisher of our faith, who for the joy that was set before Him endured the cross, despising the shame, and has sat down at the right hand of the throne of God. (Hebrews 12:1-2)

You can only attain the grave cloths through total death to self, willingly crucifying the flesh daily and bringing it into the obedience of Christ Jesus. Only dead people were wrapped in grave cloths after ritual purification. And it's only when we come to the realization that we must crucify our flesh, being dead to sin and alive in Him, we qualify to wear the shame for the body of Christ.

In Jesus's time, bodies were prepared for burial by washing them, anointing them with aromatic oils and spices like myrrh and aloes, and then wrapping them in linen strips and a burial shroud. The washing cleansed the body to prepare it for the afterlife, reflecting religious beliefs that the deceased should be holy and pure upon their return to God. After these preparations, the body was carried to a rock-hewn tomb or a grave for burial, a process that had to be completed within hours of death. (From Wikipedia)

After this, Joseph of Arimathea, being a disciple of Jesus, but secretly, for fear of the

Jews, asked Pilate that he might take away the body of Jesus; and Pilate gave him permission. So he came and took the body of Jesus. And Nicodemus, who at first came to Jesus by night, also came, bringing a mixture of myrrh and aloes, about a hundred pounds. Then they took the body of Jesus, and bound it in strips of linen with the spices, as the custom of the Jews is to bury. Now in the place where He was crucified there was a garden, and in the garden a new tomb in which no one had yet been laid. So there they laid Jesus, because of the Jews' Preparation Day, for the tomb was nearby. (John 19:38-42)

By these customary standards, I believe the sting of death (aka our sin) was washed away from the Lord. Symbolically Joseph of Arimathea first washed the Lord's body then anointed it with oil and clean linen. He then wrapped His body and placed it in his own tomb and rolled the stone over its opening.

Jesus died for us outside the city therefore our sin had to be left outside the holy sepulcher. Christ' tomb is symbolic of the womb of the anointing, the holy of holies, where sin cannot enter.

Therefore, Jesus also, that He might sanctify the people with His own

> *blood, suffered outside the gate. Therefore, let us go forth to Him, outside the camp, bearing His reproach. (Hebrews 13:12-13)*

An unclean body could not be placed in a tomb because contact with the dead or with a tomb made a person ritually impure, which was seen as a spiritual and social defilement that could prevent them from entering God's presence or participating in worship. This concept of "corpse uncleanness" is based on Old Testament law, and it required purification rituals before a person could become clean again. While burial was required for the deceased, it was understood that those involved would have to undergo a period of cleansing afterward. (Wikipedia)

Therefore, our sin nature was dead in Him on the cross. And, symbolically through the purification process the one new man was created in Him being bathed, purified and wrapped in holy garments. The tomb is like the womb of the anointing that held the one new man without sin. And there, resurrection life occurs in Christ, and we are raised to life in Him.

> *For He Himself is our peace, who has made both one, and has broken down the middle wall of separation, having abolished in His*

flesh the enmity, that is, the law of commandments contained in ordinances, so as to create in Himself one new man from the two, thus making peace, and that He might reconcile them both to God in one body through the cross, thereby putting to death the enmity. (Ephesians 2:14-16)

"It is no longer I who live but Christ who lives within me." Paul was the perfect example of living his life unto death. By all means he became a victor of the grave cloth.

CHAPTER FIVE

THE MARTYR'S ROBE

Thou shall not kill, says the Martyr!

Here is another conversation with the Lord. This time He's speaking about the martyr's robe and the importance of wearing it.

As you wear the martyr's robe you understand what this means. You can kill with your words; character assassination is more deadly than the bullet. Why? The bullet is fatal while the character dies a slow death.

When you wear the Martyrs' robe, you've crossed the line of no return. You've determined in your mind and soul that you will not return to the system of man and compromise the cross. Why? The cross is eternal life and apart from it is death, eternal.

Homosexual Desire Dishonors the Robe

Many have tried it on for pleasure. They talk as if they are committed but when things shake their faith, they quickly turn back, walking away in shame and guilt yet some dishonor the robe by homosexual desire. Do you know how many Christians are homosexuals? *No, Lord, I don't and I'm asking, can a Christian be a homosexual since it's an abomination according to scripture.*

Note: Let me stop here and say, I was surprised the Lord asked me this question in the midst of our conversation. But since He did, I responded with a question. Here are my supporting scriptures.

> *You shall not lie with a male as with a woman. It is an abomination. (Leviticus 18:22)*

> *If a man lies with a male as he lies with a woman, both of them have committed an abomination. They shall surely be put to death. Their blood shall be upon them. (Leviticus 20:13)*

I felt it was important to add this sections since it's obviously important to the Lord. I believe the hypocrisy in the current church age lays heavy on the heart of the Father. Homosexuality is a choice. Perhaps what the Lord is saying is that when someone in ministry has an unnatural sexual desire instead of them crucifying their flesh, they take the easy road and give into it. And this would include adultery and fornication. Remember God told Cain, that sin lies at the door, and its desire is for you, but you should rule over it." (Genesis 4:7) That's the moment of decision and it will determine the direction your life takes. Will you rule over it and walk with God or give in to its temptation and walk the way of the flesh.

> *Do you not know that the unrighteous will not inherit the kingdom of God? Do not be deceived. Neither fornicators, nor idolaters, nor adulterers, nor homosexuals, nor sodomites, nor thieves, nor covetous, nor drunkards, nor revilers, nor extortioners will inherit the kingdom of God. (1 Corinthians 6:9-10)*

The Lord Continued,
Many homosexuals have turned away from that lifestyle never to return yet some go back to it and never return to Me. But a homosexual cannot be a Christian. Christian life does not mean one sex; man to man or woman to woman. I created man to be with a woman and a woman with a man. Anything other than that is an abomination. A homosexual can come clean through repentance, and I forgive them. But a Christian cannot participate in such activities.

Note: I want to address a few things Bob and I used to discuss before moving on to the rest of what God is saying regarding the martyr's robe.

All sin is against God yet man categorizes it. We begin with 613 laws of Moses found in the Torah. They were condensed to the 10 Commandments. And still, no one could keep them. If you broke one, you were guilty of breaking them all. We now have one Law and that is to love God, your neighbor and yourself.

> *Teacher, which is the great commandment in the law? Jesus said to him, "You shall love the LORD your God with all your heart, with all your soul, and with all your mind. This is the first and great commandment. And the second is like it: You shall love your neighbor as yourself." (Matthew 22:36-39)*

Bob was very emphatic about people in sexual relations outside of marriage. He said, "If you have a loved one, who's participating in a sexual sin and you don't tell them the truth, you're condemning their soul to eternal damnation."

Some people have never heard the gospel. Many people have Bibles but don't read them. It's possible that many sit in darkness because they don't know or understand what the scripture says regarding sexual sin yet scripture is very clear.

I believe that church leaders who ordain homosexual pastors and leaders, as well as and those who perform same-sex marriages are guilty of the abomination of this sin. And they will answer to Almighty God for their actions. When a homosexual or adulterous leader ministers out of a defiled conscience they release an ungodly spirit to everyone in the sound of their voice. And they will be held accountable for misleading, misguiding, miscommunicating and defiling God's precious and holy word.

Where is the Martyr's Robe

**Back to what the Lord was saying about the martyr's robe.

Bonnie, where is the martyr's robe right now? *I don't know Lord, what do you mean? Who is wearing it?* Donald Trump.

He has laid his life down, over and over and allowed Me to use his voice to crucify man's flesh. Why do you think the media attacks him continuously? Character assassination is far worse, more brutal than the bullet. Watch and see what I do in the following year to turn this nation around.

According to Webster's Dictionary a "martyr" is a person who voluntarily suffers death as the penalty for declaring belief in and refusing to renounce a religion. It is also a person who sacrifices something of great value and especially life itself for the sake of principle.

Stephen the Martyr

Stephen is the first Christian martyr in scripture. As the story unfolds in Acts Chapter 6, in order for the apostles to continue ministering the gospel, they appointed 7 men of good reputation, full of the Holy Spirit and wisdom, to care for the Hellenistic widows because they were neglected in the daily distribution. (Acts 6:1-4)

Stephen, a man of great faith and power, performed great signs and wonders. This greatly disturbed the members of the Synagogue of the Freedmen. They couldn't resist his wisdom given by Holy Spirit. And the word of God spread, and the number of the disciples multiplied greatly in Jerusalem, and a great many of the priests were obedient to the faith. (Acts 6:8-10)

Unable to silence him, they convinced others to report hearing Stephen say blasphemous words against Moses and God, destroying the holy place and changing the law of Moses. They accused him unjustly. Yet all who sat in the council, looking steadfastly at him, saw his face as the face of an angel. (Acts 6:12-15) When the high priest said, "Are these things so?" (Acts 7:1) Stephen began a lengthy dissertation beginning with Abraham, the Patriarchs and Moses.

And continuing forward condemned their disobedience toward God saying;

> *"You stiff-necked and uncircumcised in heart and ears! You always resist the Holy Spirit; as your fathers did, so do you. Which of the prophets did your fathers not persecute? And they killed those who foretold the coming of the Just One, of whom you now have become the betrayers and murderers, who have received the law by the direction of angels and have not kept it." When they heard these things, they were cut to the heart, and they gnashed at him with their teeth. (7:51-54)*

Stephen, like Joshua and Calab, was of another spirit. (Numbers 14:24) He was filled with Holy Spirit, boldness and power. But he, being full of the Holy Spirit, gazed into heaven and saw the glory of God, and Jesus standing at the right hand of God, and said, "Look! I see the heavens opened and the Son of Man standing at the right hand of God!" (Acts 7:55-57)

Driving Stephen out of the city, like they did to Jesus, they cried out with a loud voice, stopped their ears, and ran at him with one accord; and they cast him out of the city and stoned him. And the witnesses laid down their clothes at the feet of a young man named Saul. And they stoned Stephen as he was calling on God and saying, "Lord Jesus, receive my spirit." Then he knelt down and cried out with a loud voice, "Lord, do not charge them with this sin." And when he had said this, he fell asleep. (Acts 7:57-60)

Because they didn't agree with Stephen's teachings and didn't know how to combat him with truth, they wrongly accused him and called him a blasphemer while trying to discredit him. This was character assassination and most importantly they were blaspheming against Holy Spirit. They already killed him with their words. Now the stones were their final blow.

Who's Wearing the Martyr's Robe Right Now

The Lord asked me, "Where is the martyr's robe right now?" And I answered with a question. *Who is wearing it?"* His response, "Donald Trump." Yes, I agree, as you can see in the past 10 years, time after time Donald Trump was in the midst of a media frenzy continuously attacked on all fronts. Only by the grace of God did he maintain a steadfast attitude. Often times he spoke things that sounded rather unkind. Yet he was truthful in his response to the mainstream media's constant attacks.

The Lord said character assassination is a slow death. It's like a little cyanide over a long period of time will kill you. An assassin's bullet is quick because it's done and over. But a lingering death by character assassination over and over is quite painful. Yet the Lord has used Donald Trump many times to bring forth His Kingdom's message, His truth and His justice. I would agree Donald Trump wears the martyr's robe because he allows the Lord to lift up His voice to tear down governmental strongholds.

In fact, I believe God commissioned Donald Trump like He did Jeremiah. He ordained Donald John Trump from his mother's womb and sanctified him and ordained him a prophet to the nations of the world. And in his years in political authority, he would root out and pull down, destroy and throw down, build and plant."

> *Before I formed you in the womb I knew you; before you were born, I sanctified you; I ordained you a prophet to the nations. (Jeremiah 1:5)*
>
> *Then the LORD put forth His hand and touched my mouth, and the LORD said to me: "Behold, I have put My words in*

your mouth. See, I have this day set you over the nations and over the kingdoms, to root out and to pull down, to destroy and to throw down, to build and to plant." (Jeremiah 1:9-10)

My question is to the body of Christ, are you willing to wear the martyr robe? Are you willing to take the hits from the enemy on all sides? Many of the assassinations come from within the church. Will you be the one to cast a stone at your brother? Or will you walk in the Jeremiah anointing? Will you stand up for the sake of the gospel like Steven? Will you defend the cross of Christ? Who is worthy to wear the martyr's robe?

Thou shall not kill, says the martyr; is the command that began this chapter. Love is the only antidote to the assassin's bullet and character assassination. Remember Stephen's act of unconditional love. *Then he knelt down and cried out with a loud voice, "Lord, do not charge them with this sin." And when he had said this, he fell asleep. (Acts 7:60)*

Summary

Then He said to His disciples, "The harvest truly is plentiful, but the laborers are few. Therefore, pray the Lord of the harvest to send out laborers into His harvest." (Matthew 9:37-38)

I believe this is the heart of the Father, reaching out to His children. We are in the greatest time of harvest the world has ever known. But where are the harvesters? It is time for the body of Christ to arise, and shine, and go forth into the harvest. Every place you step is your harvest field and it's time for the glory of the Lord to rest up on His body. (Isaiah 60:1)

He's placed His words in the bride's mouth and given her authority to speak; rooting out the truth and pulling down heaven to earth, to build and plant His Kingdom. (Jeremiah 1:9-10) He's been weeding out, plucking up and removing all matters of offense so the pure bride emerges from the ashes.

For the time has come for judgment to begin at the house of God; and if it begins with us first, what will be the end of those who do not obey the gospel of God? (1 Peter 4:17)

The Father is offering two mantles this year. One is the shame of the grave cloth and the other is the martyr's robe. Each have great rewards however they will cost you everything. Who is willing to wear them? That is the question the Father is asking.

Today the "Door of Expectation" is open wide for all who dare to believe for the extraordinary! Will you dare to believe for the miraculous? Will you call those things that are not into the NOW by faith? These things have long awaited a generation of believers; those who are willing to believe beyond their imagination for the greater works Jesus talked about. Can you dare to believe? The time is NOW! There is NO HESITATION OR DELAYS!

> *"Most assuredly, I say to you, he who believes in Me, the works that I do he will do also; and greater works than these he will do, because I go to My Father. (John 14:12)*

Get ready for the journey of your lifetime as you enter through the "Door of Expectation."

Bonnie Jones

Bonnie is a good listener. She listens to God in all the ways He speaks to her. She brings a relevant word from the Lord to us in these confusing times. Bonnie's been called to spearhead "Daughters of the Dawn", a ministry geared to bring believers into bridal intimacy with the Lover of the Ages. Her walk with the Lord exemplifies what she teaches. She's a fearless prophetic voice that speaks to the body of Christ to set the captives free and transform our thinking. Among her books are The Power of the Spoken Word and Did You Learn to Love, which elaborates on Bob Jones' death experience in 1975. You can contact her to schedule a speaking engagement at contact@bonniejones.org

Made in the USA
Coppell, TX
28 January 2026

70220454R00036